A Cup Of Love

Valentine's Day Coloring Book

Your Love

Your Way

Just Color It

Anny Will

Happy Coloring

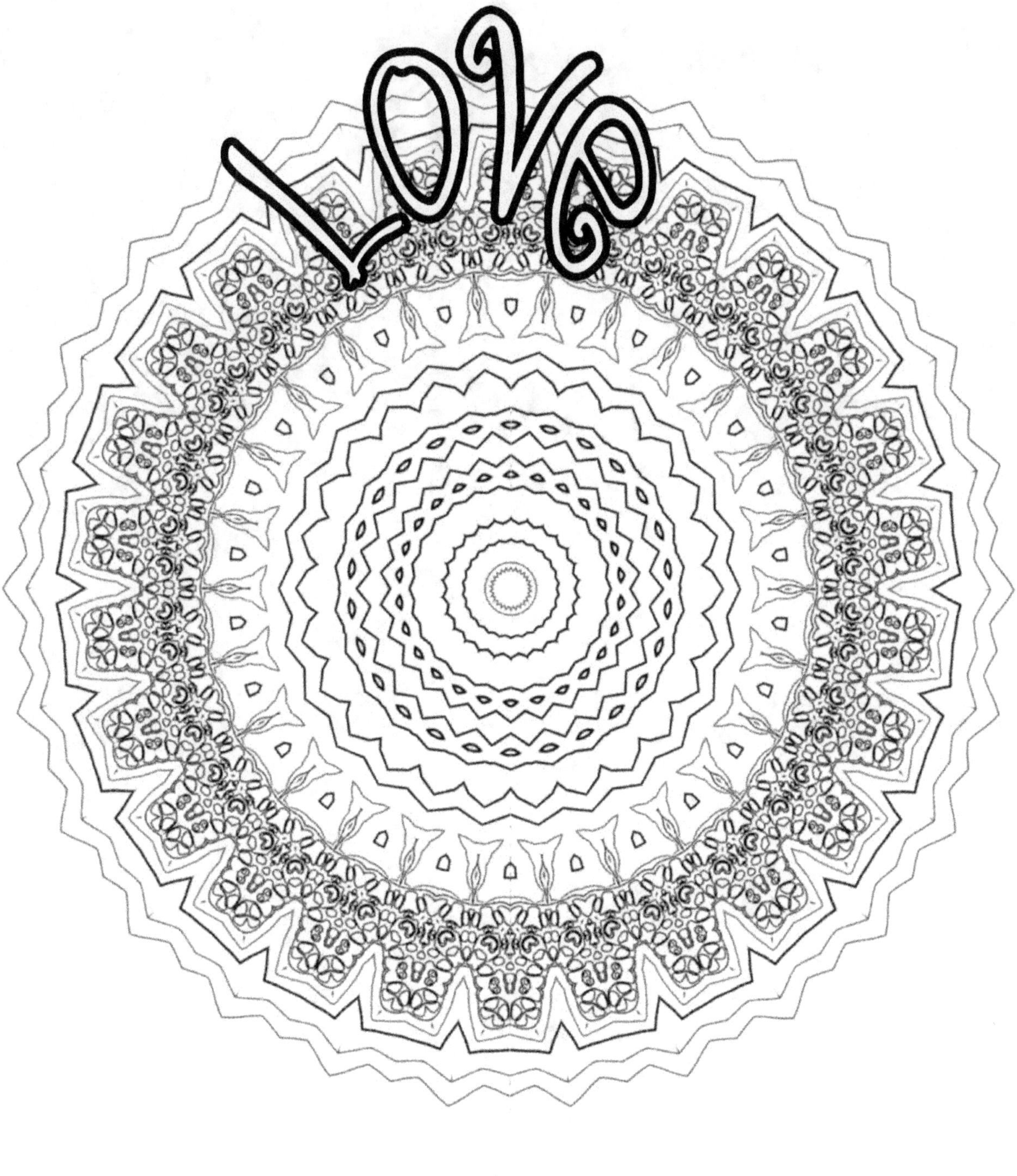
Love

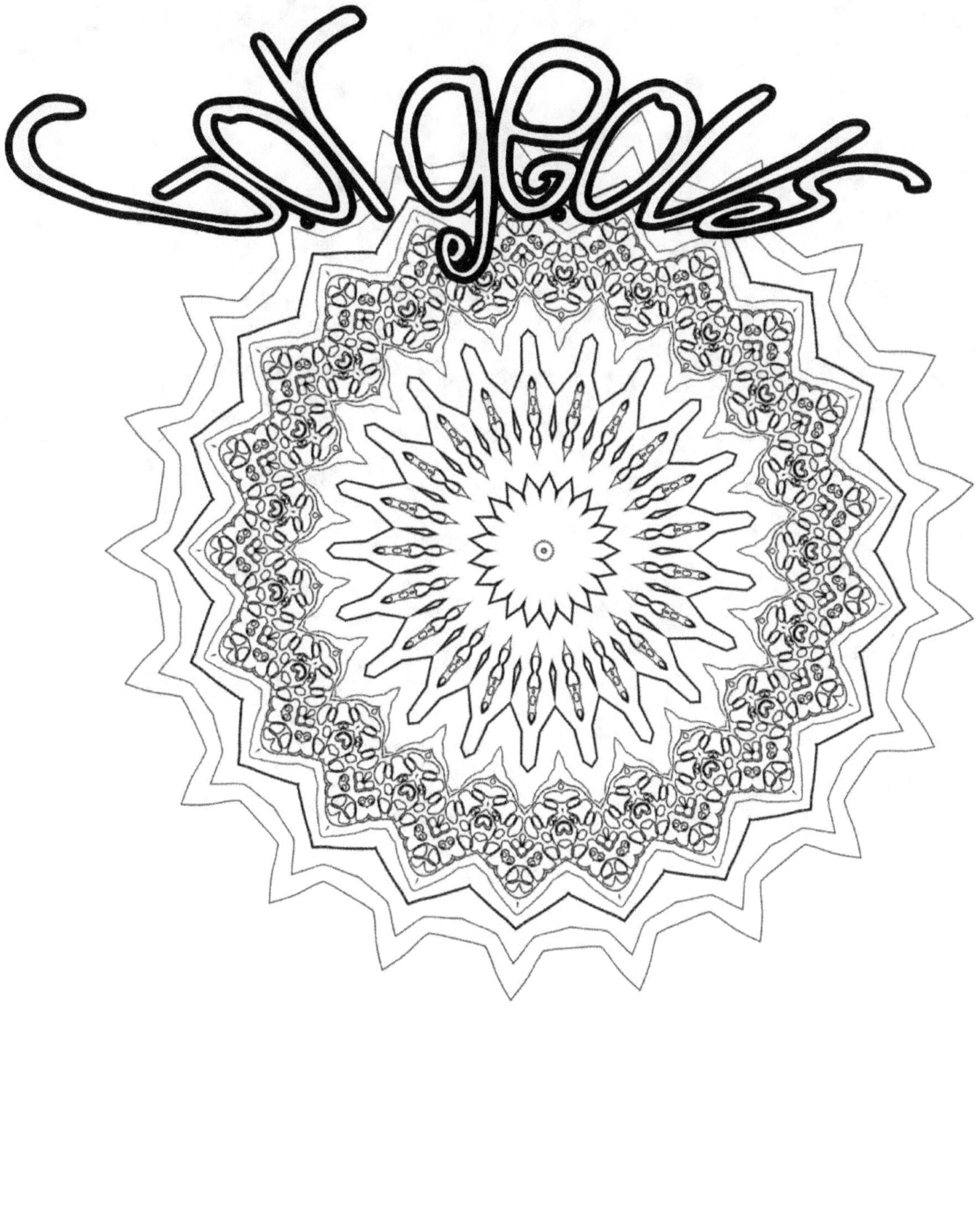

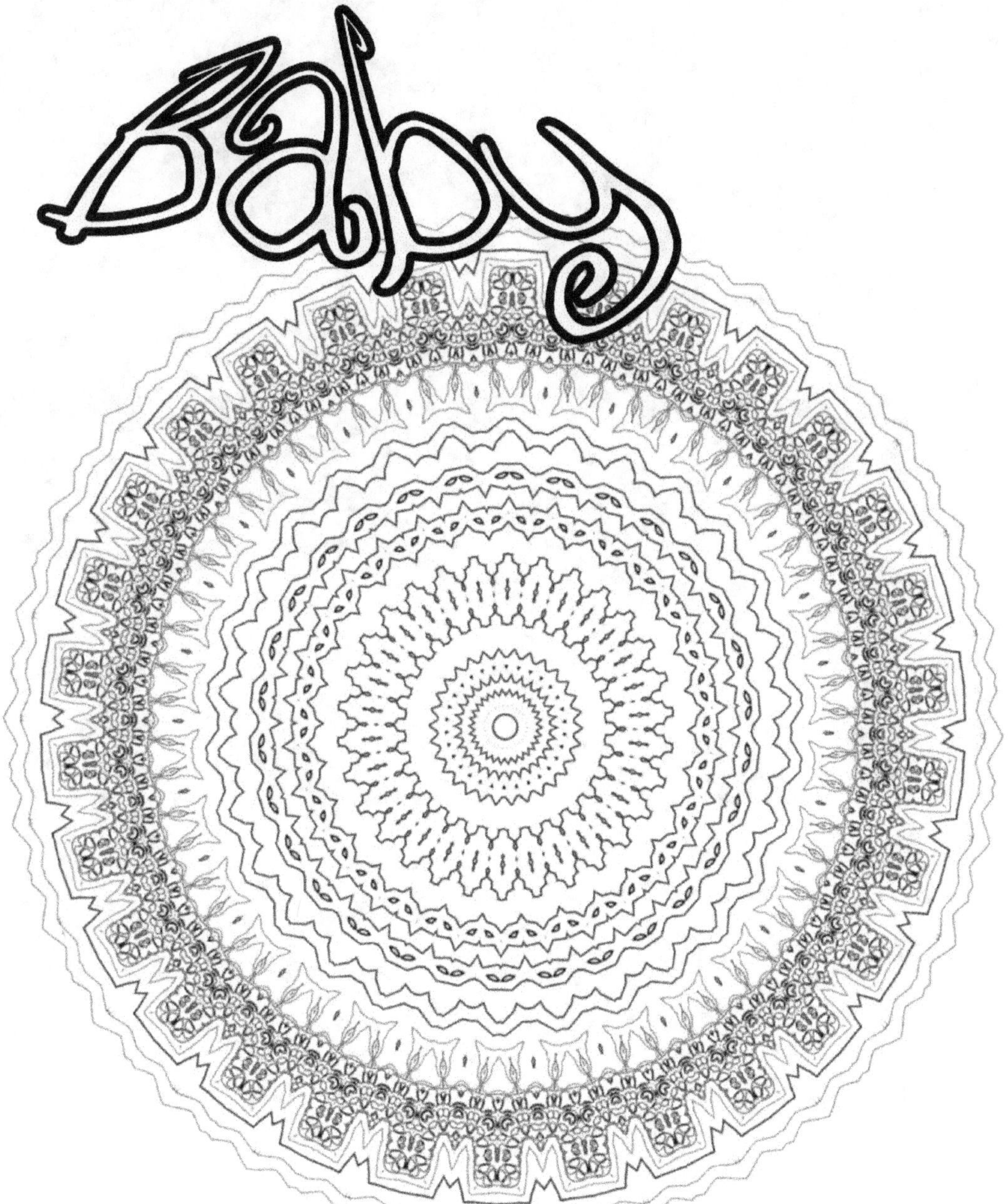
Baby

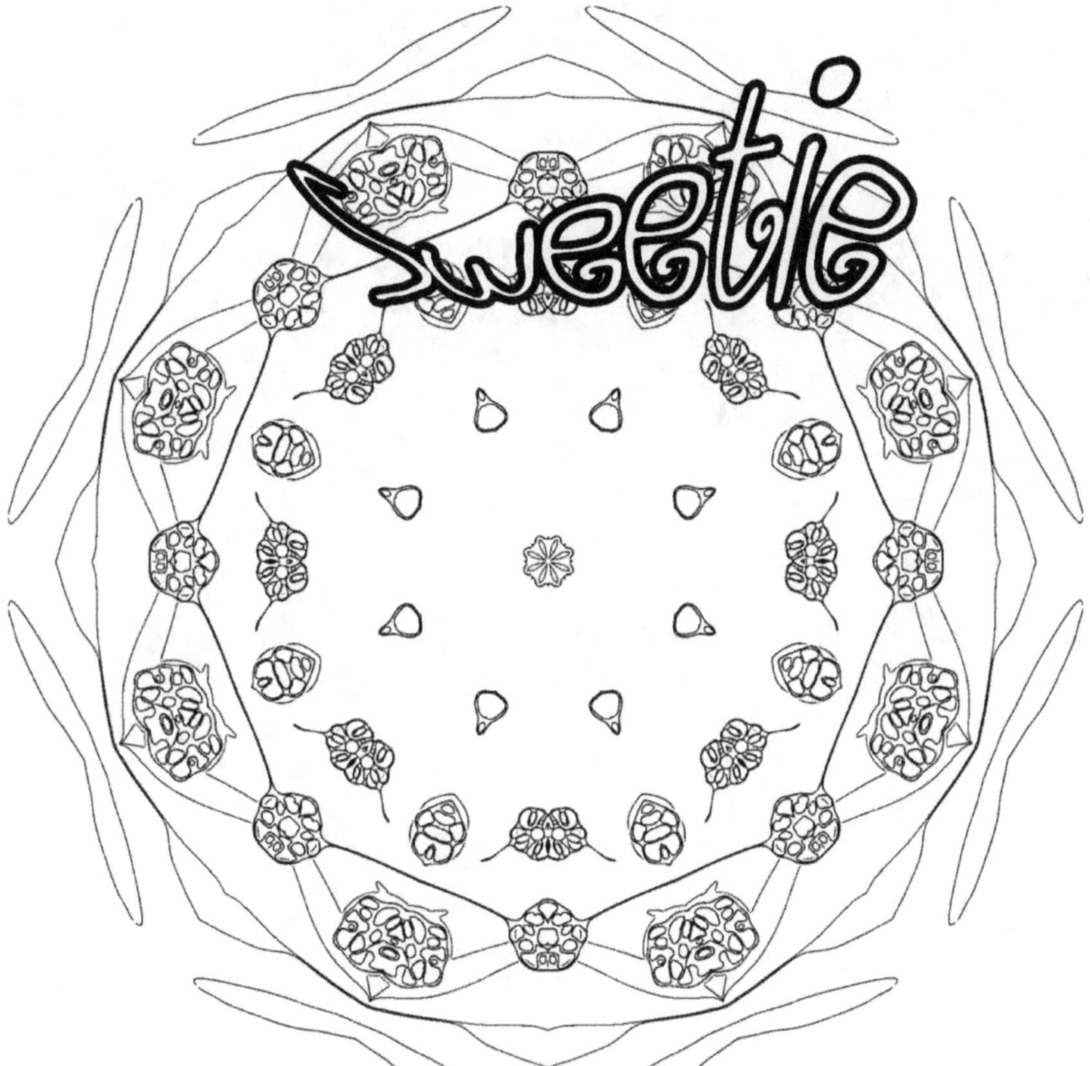
Sweetie

My Love

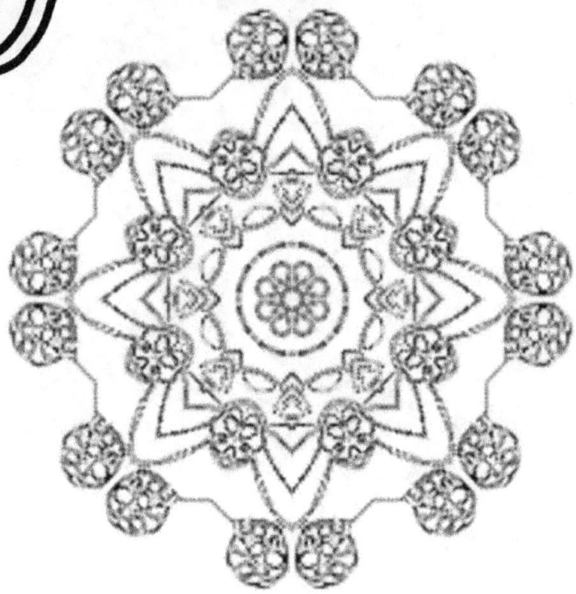

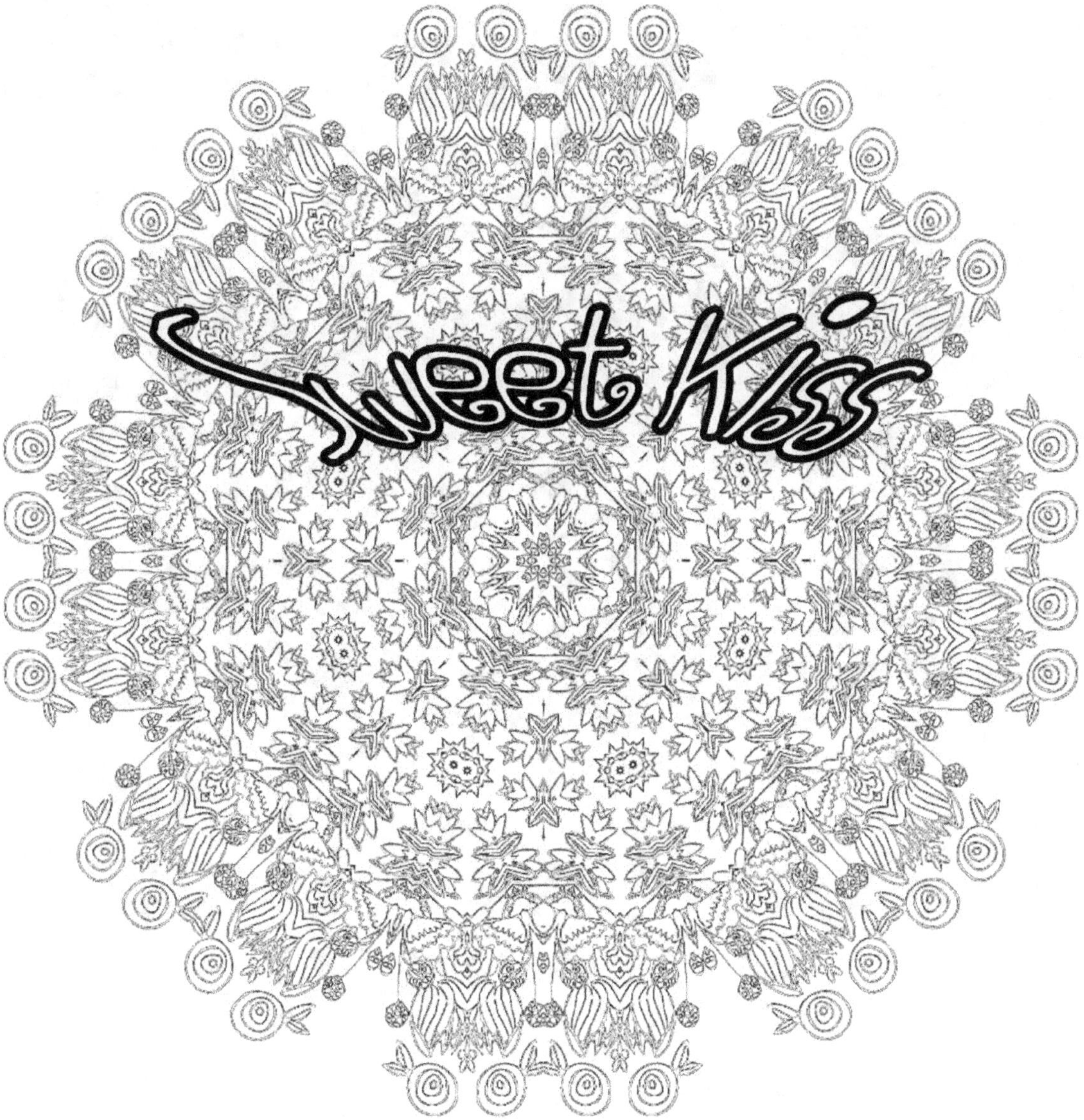
Sweet Kiss

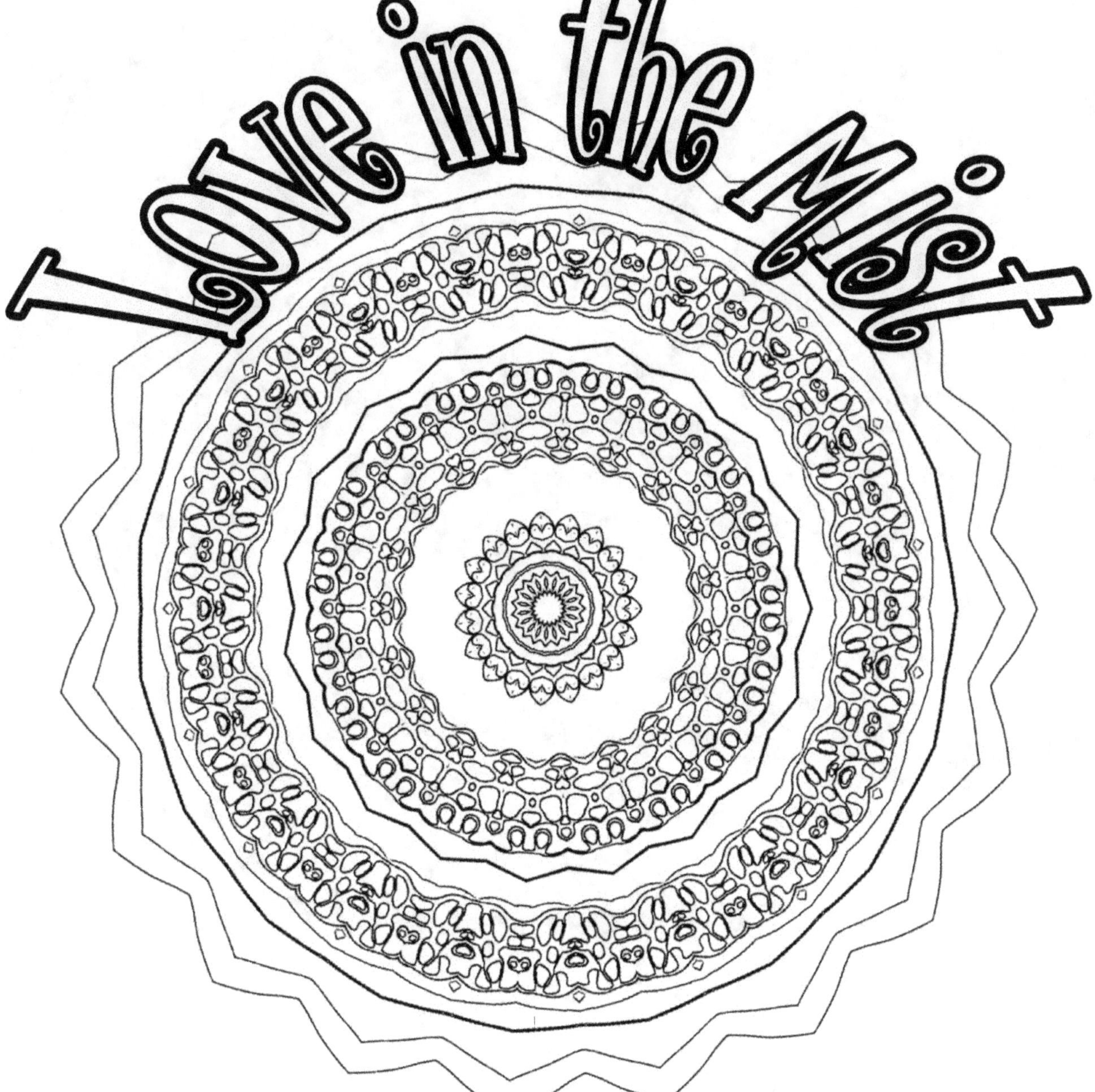
Love in the Mist

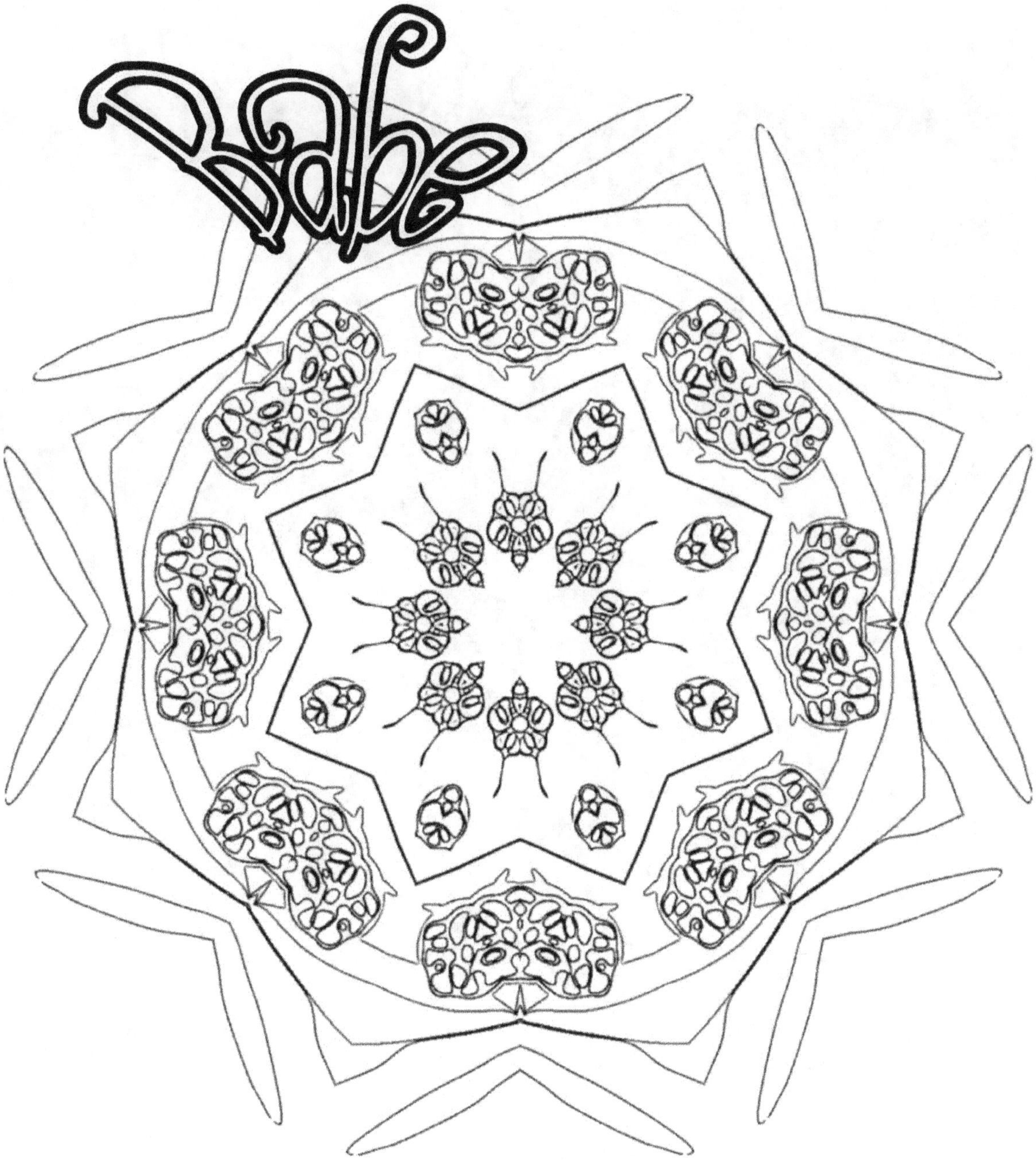
Babe

WISHING YOU

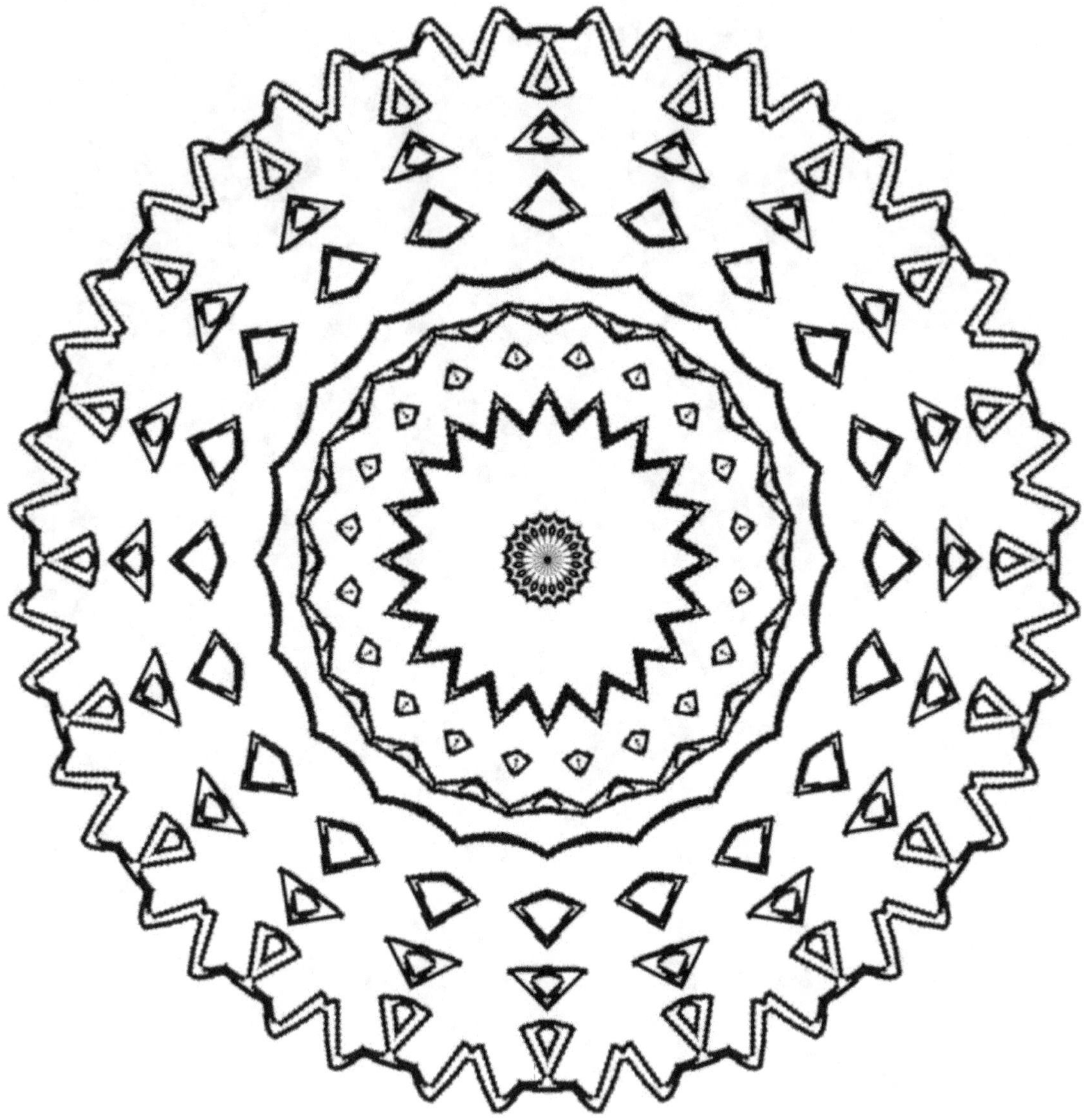

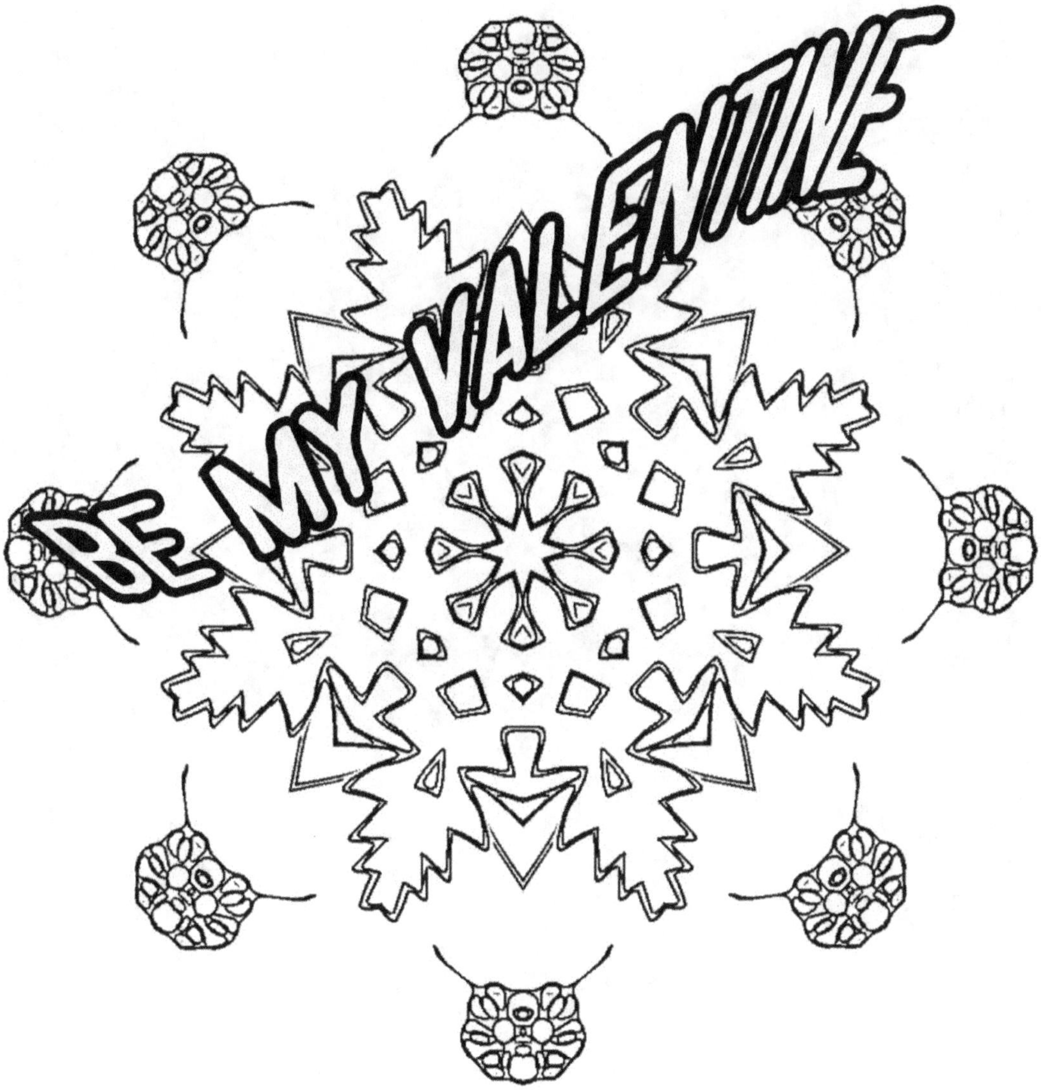
BE MY VALENITINE

SWEETHEART

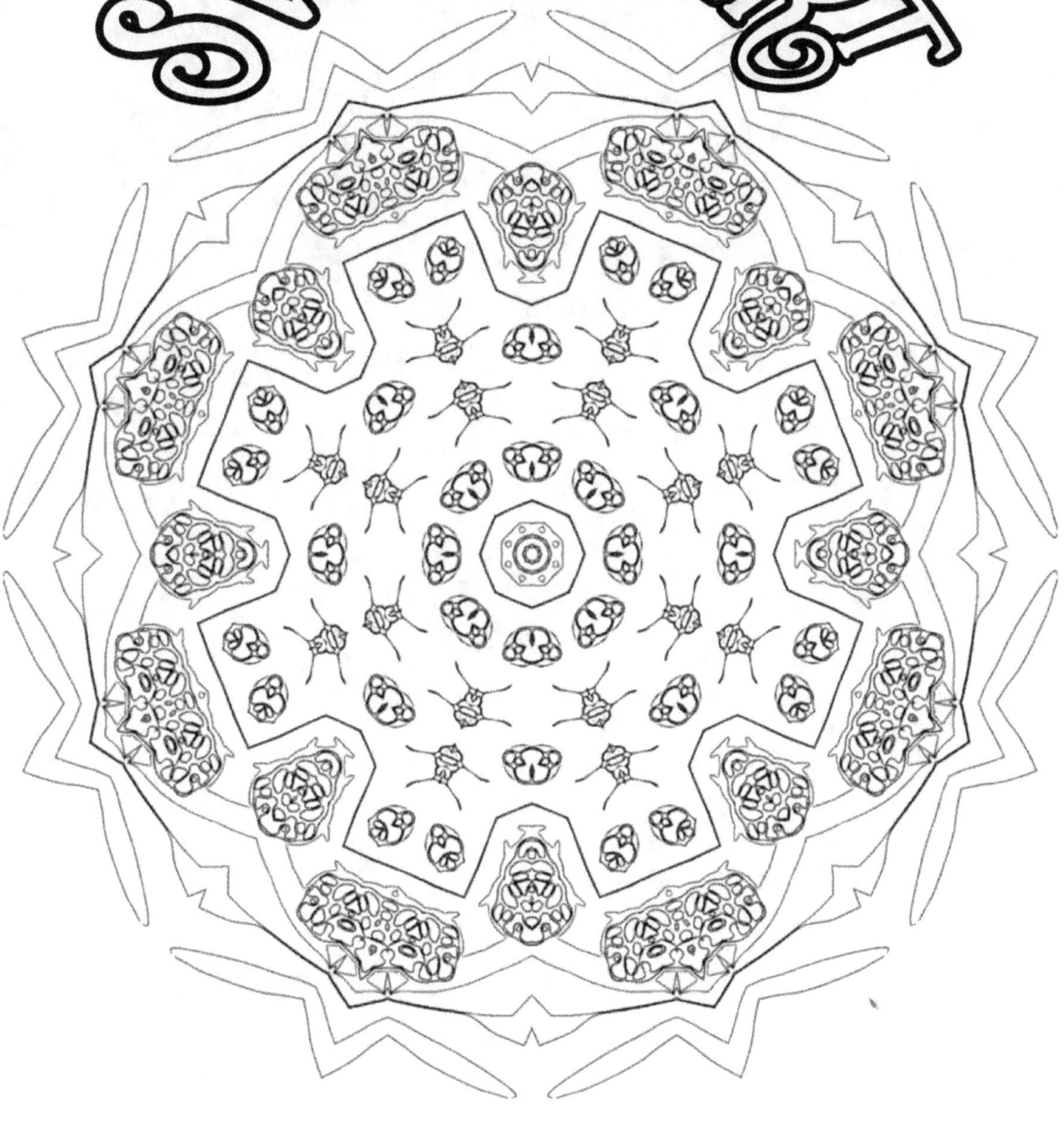

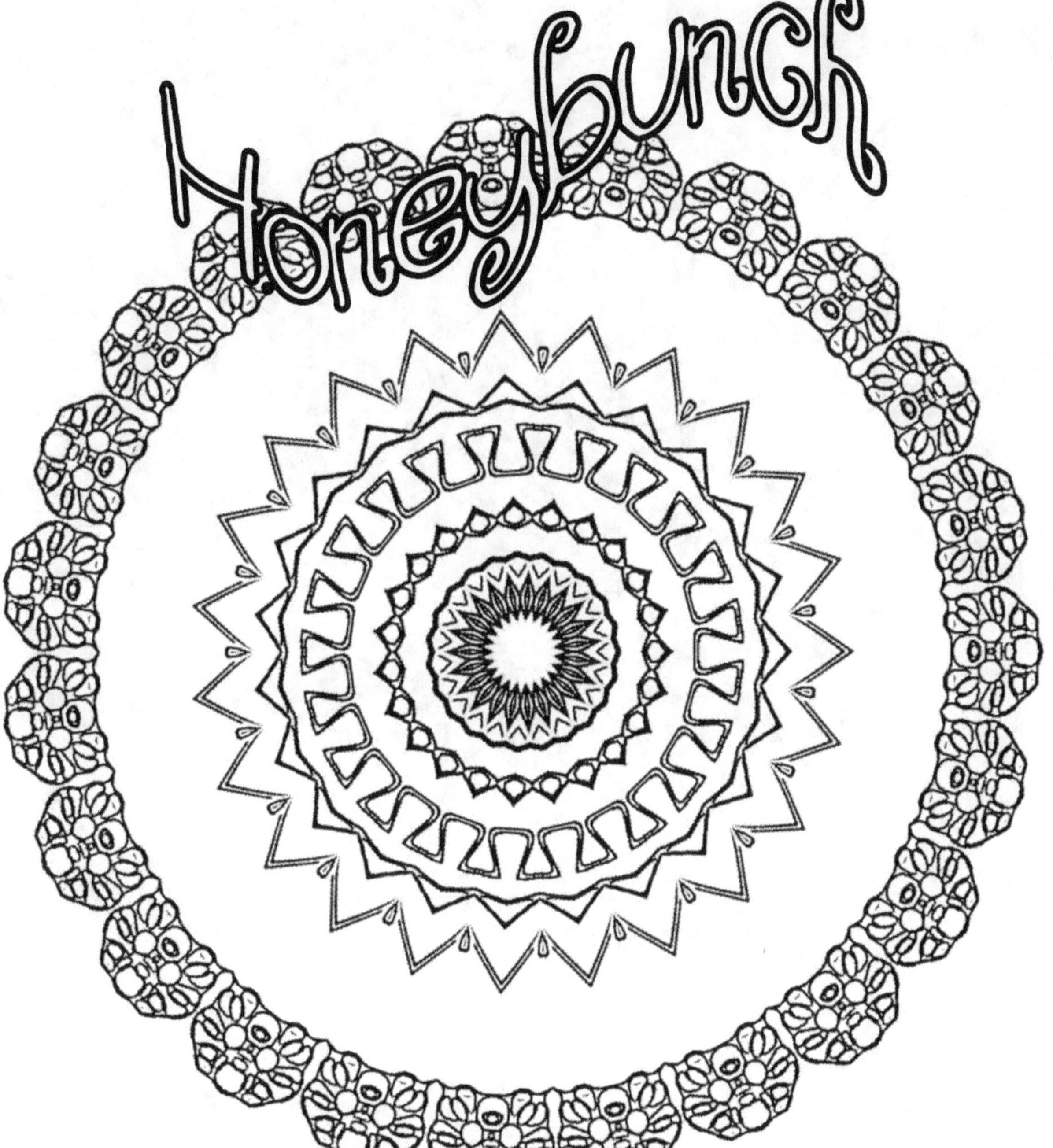
Honeybunch

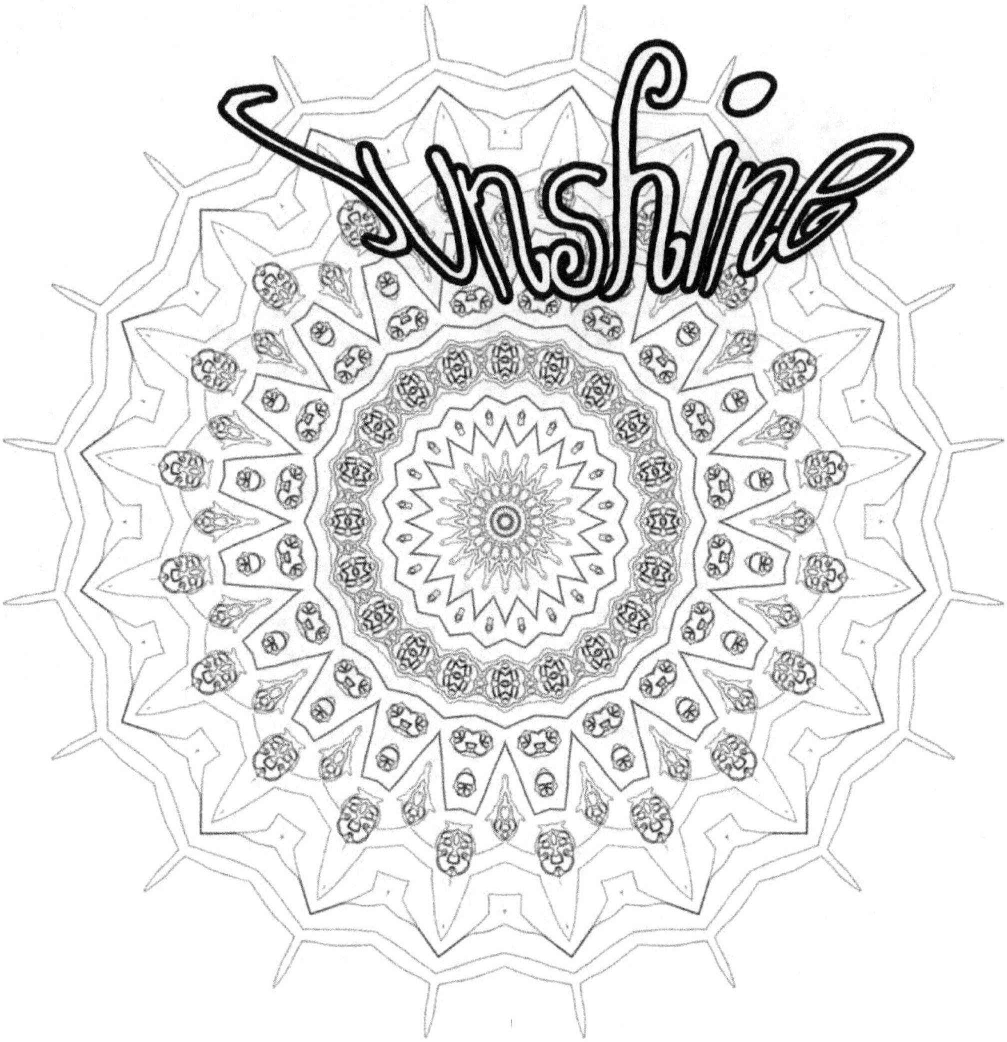
Sunshine

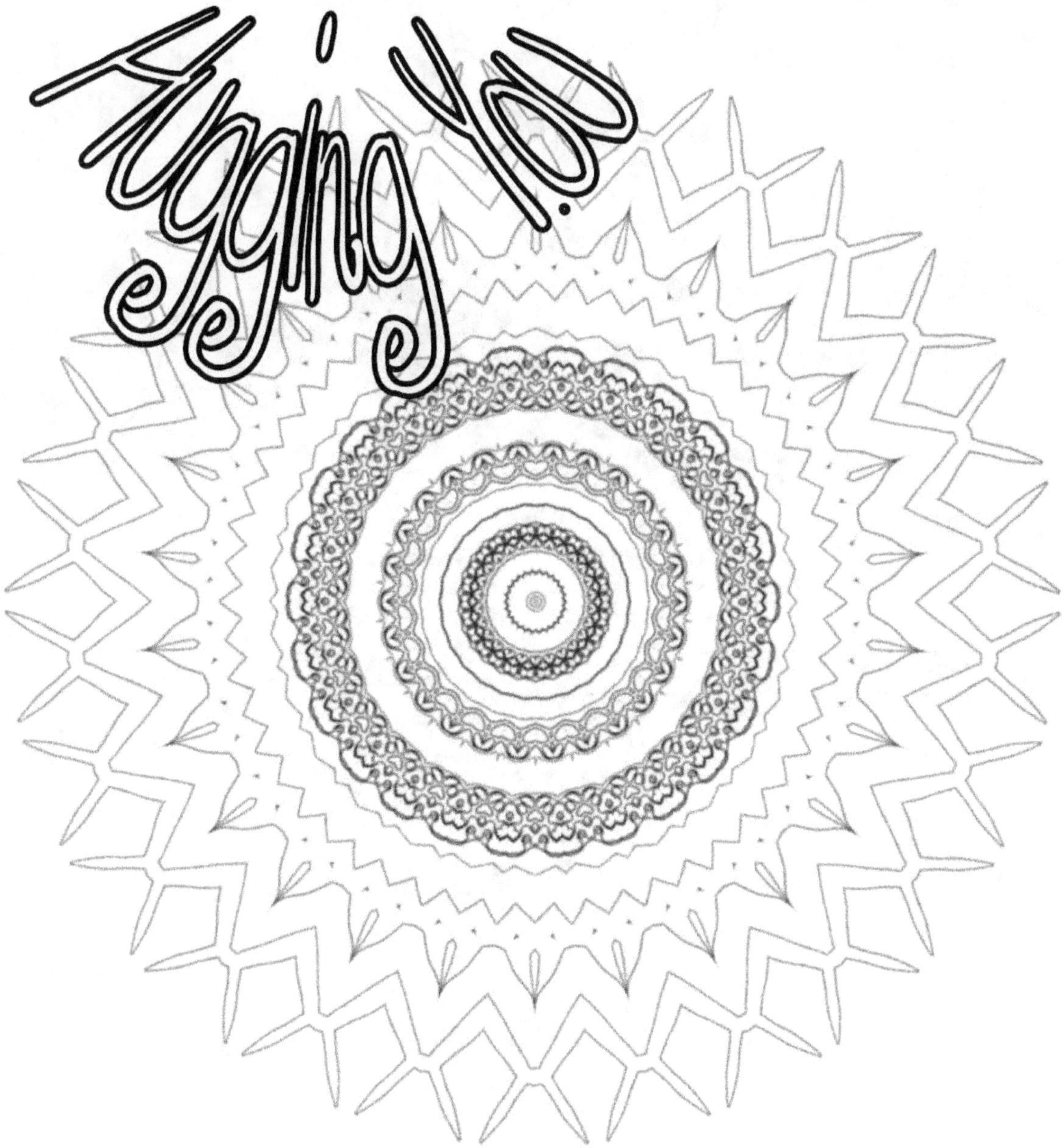
Hugging You

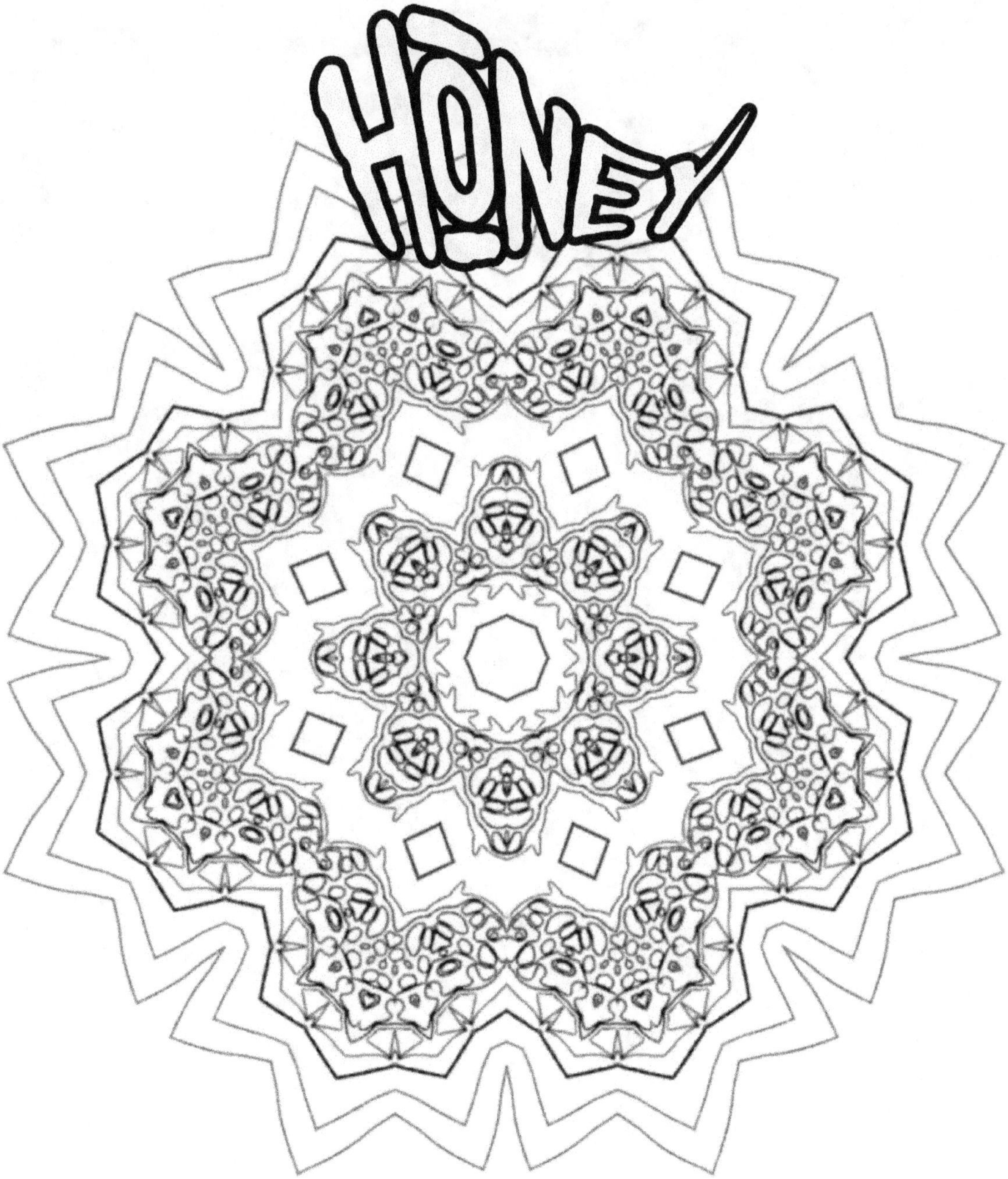
HONEY

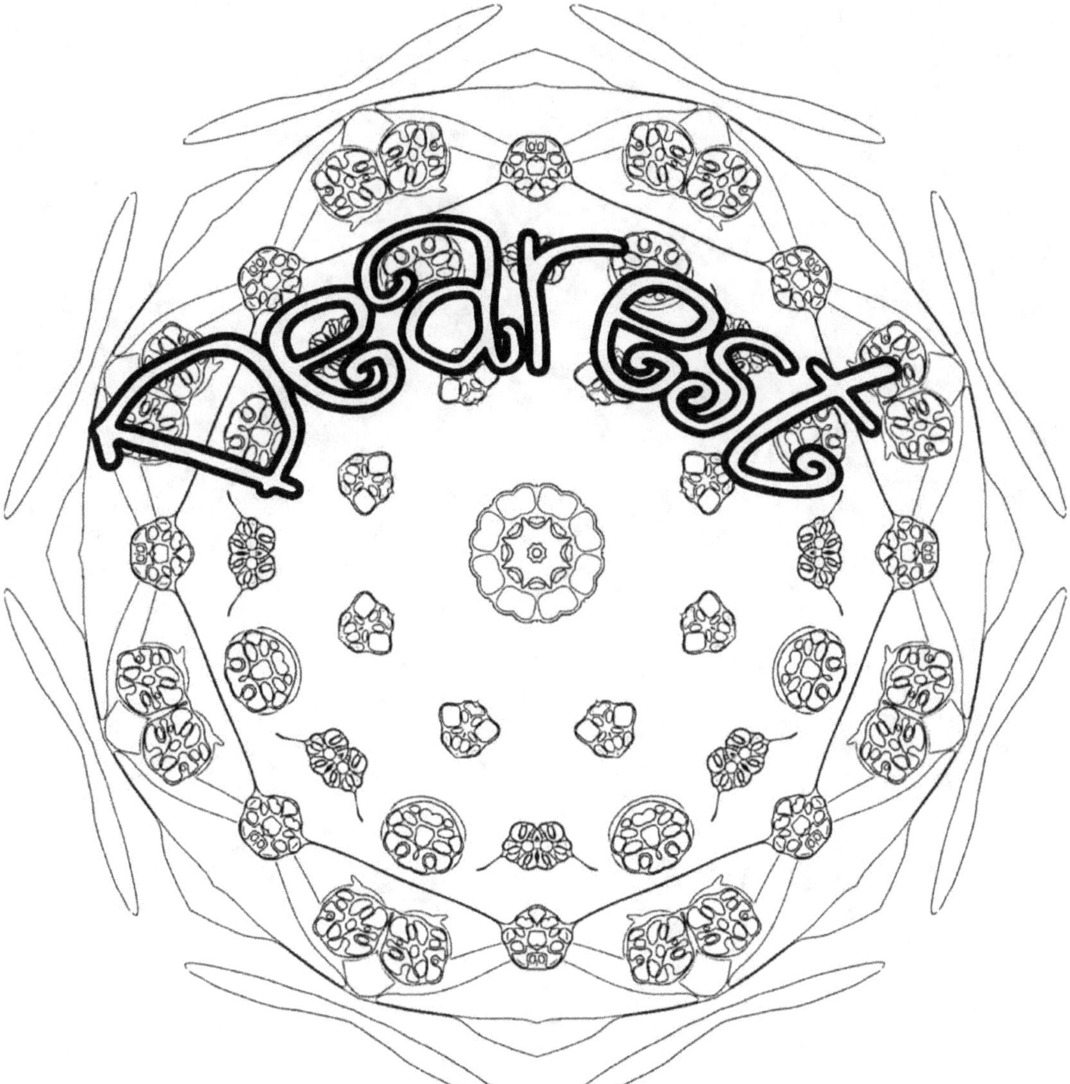
Dearest

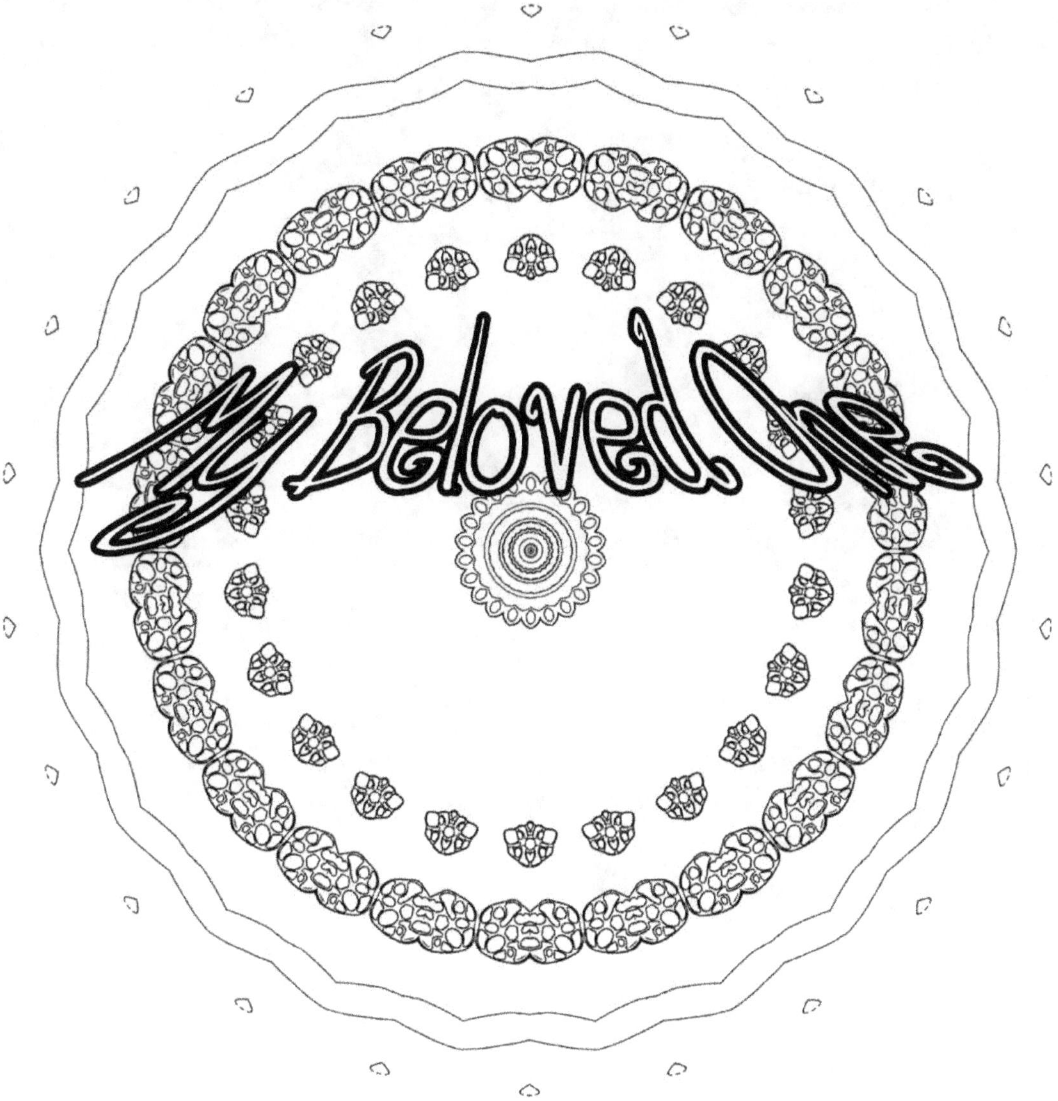
My Beloved One

The Melody of Love

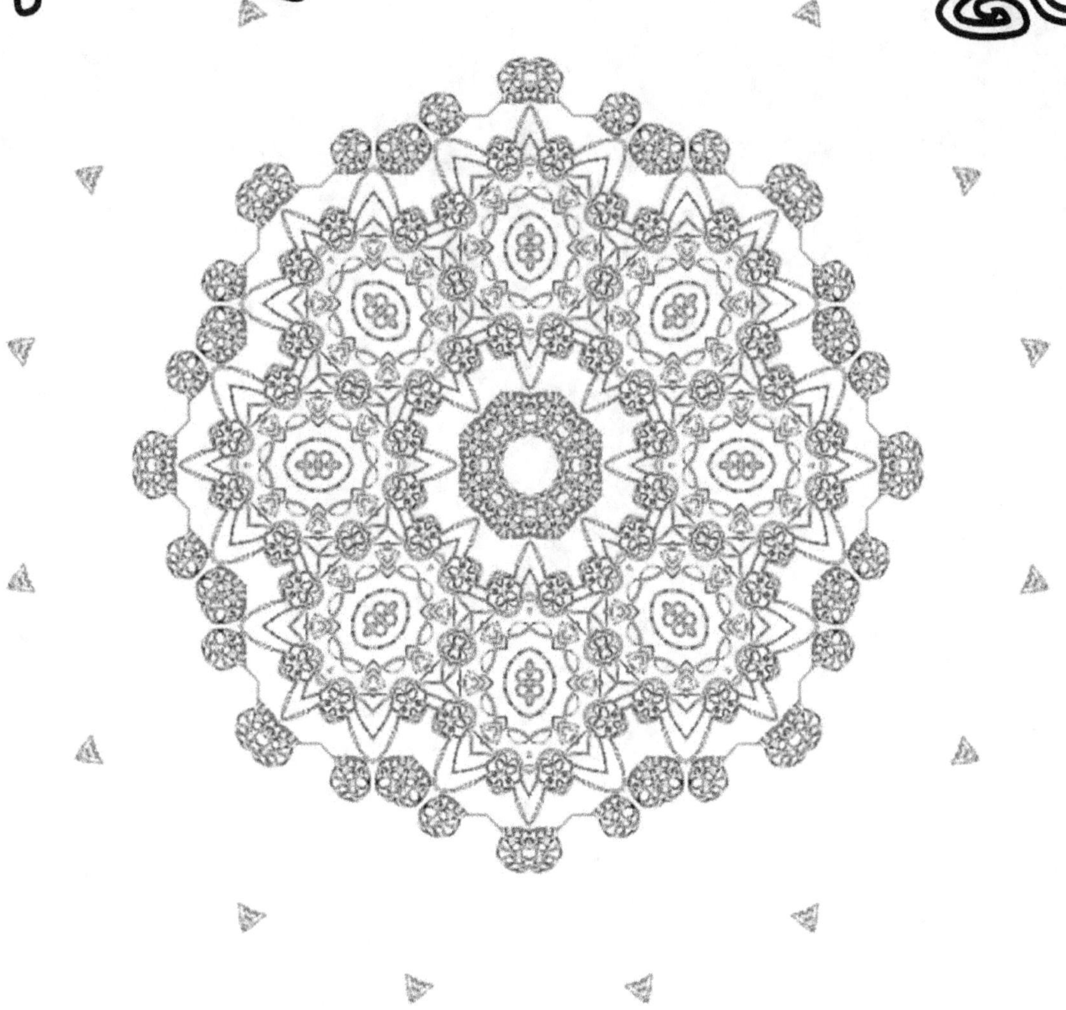

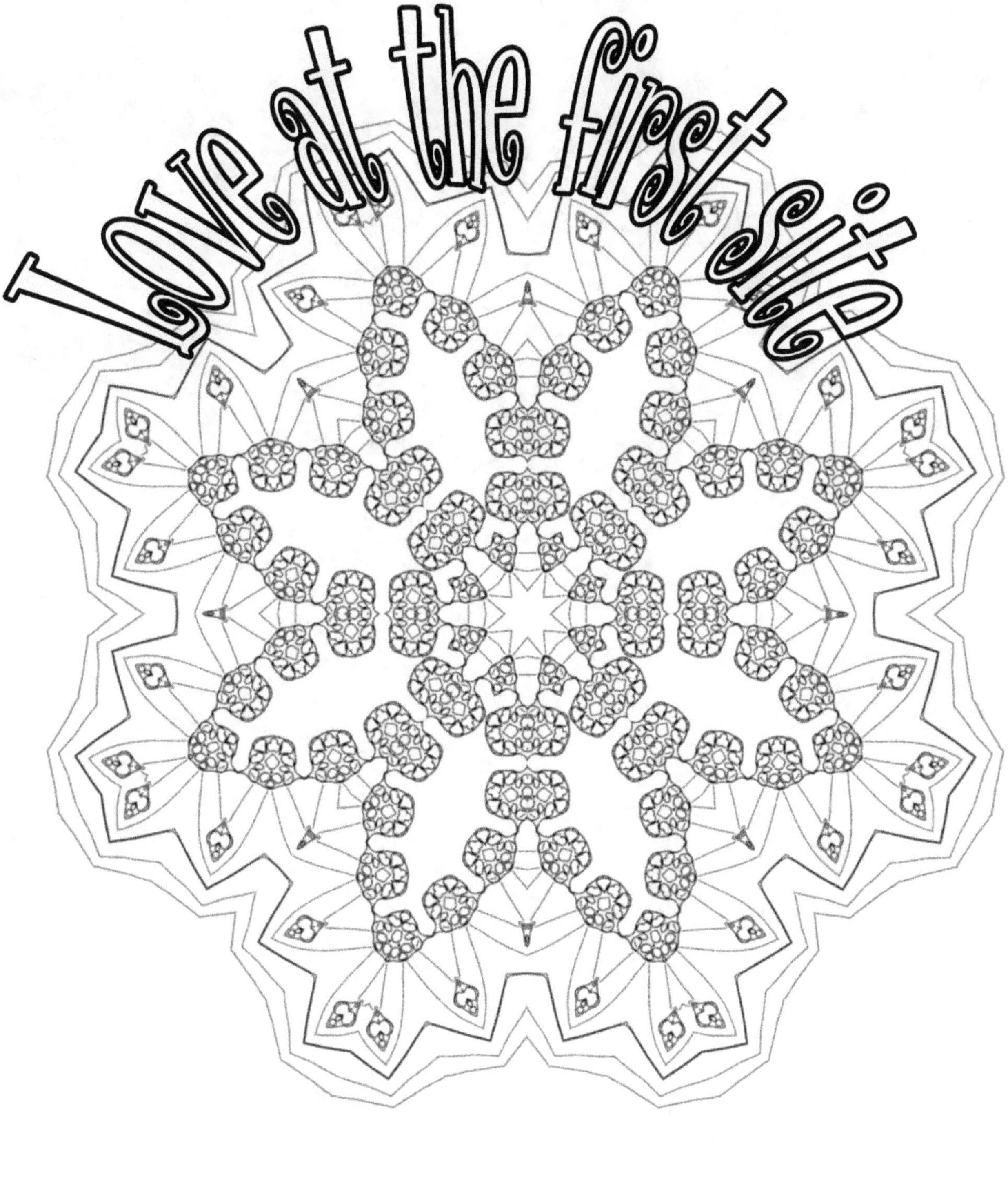
love at the first site

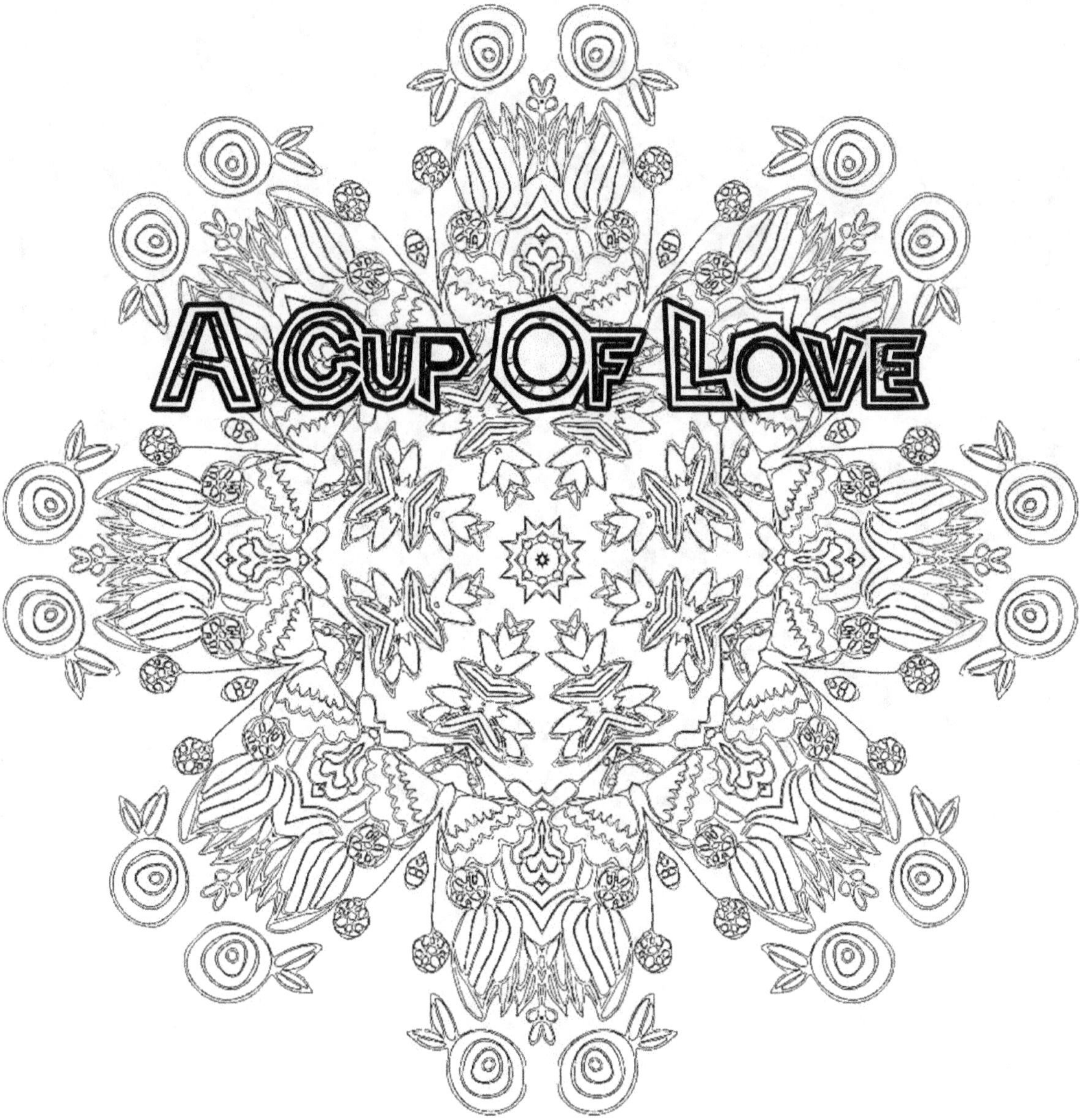
A Cup Of Love

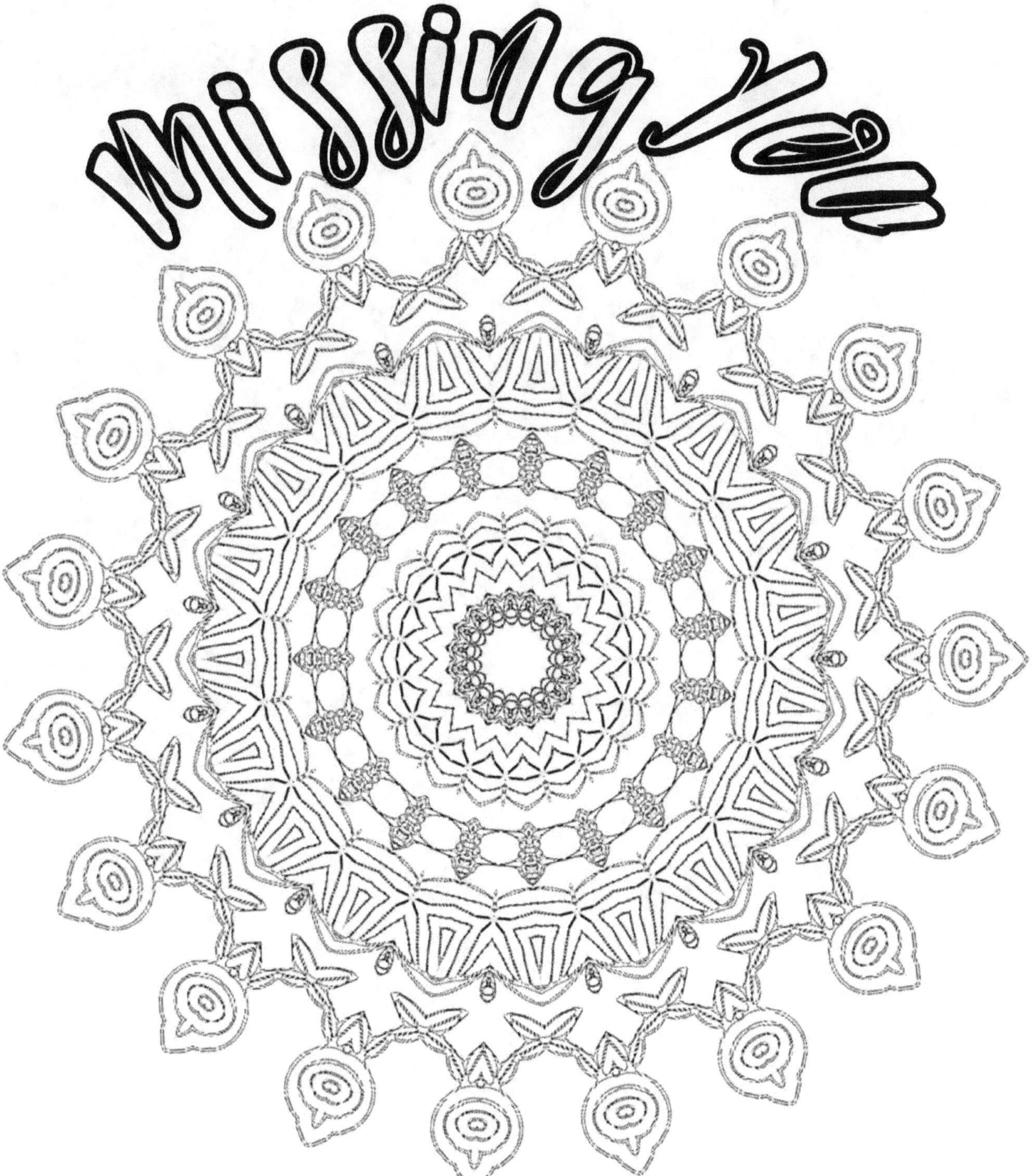
Missing You

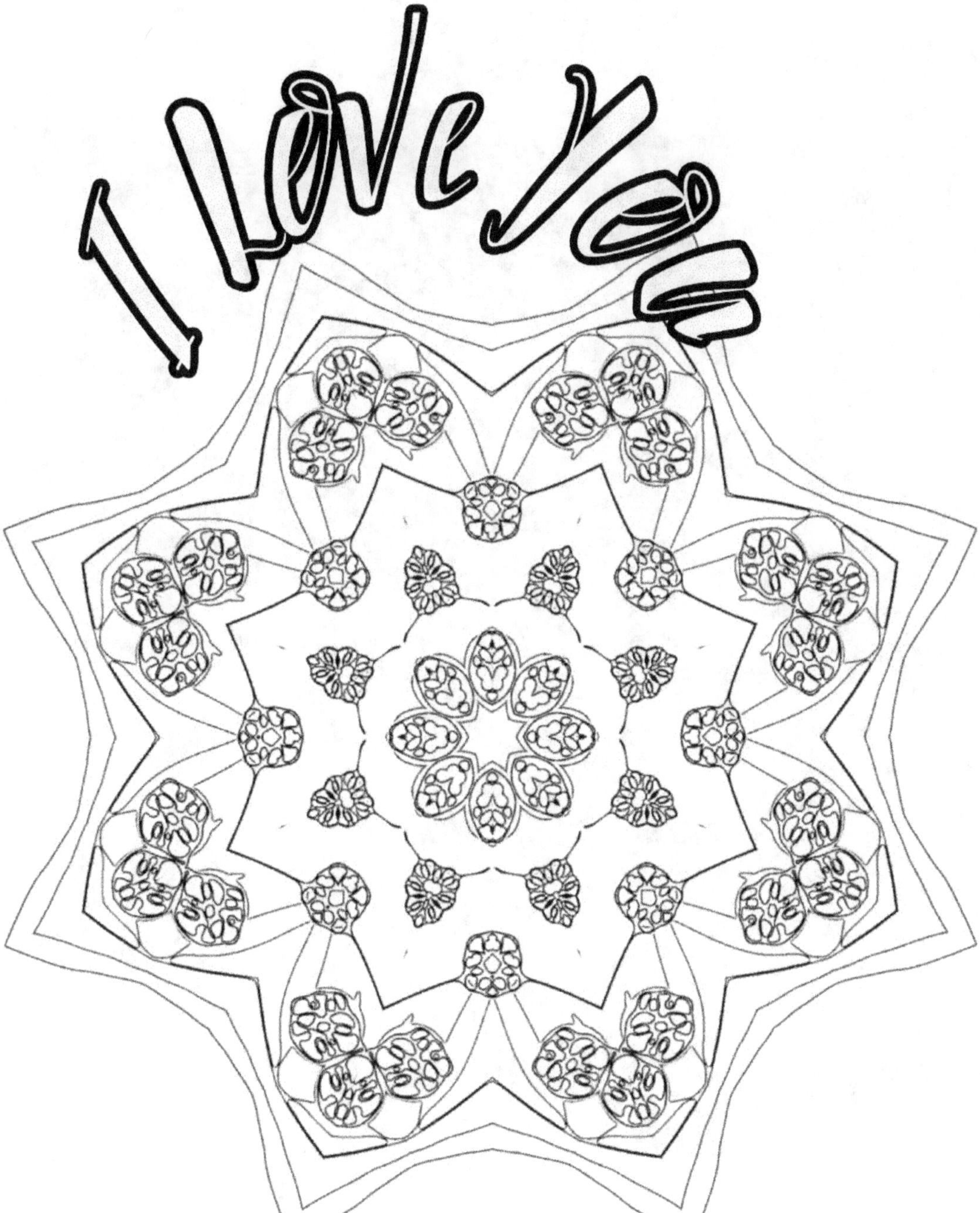
I Love You

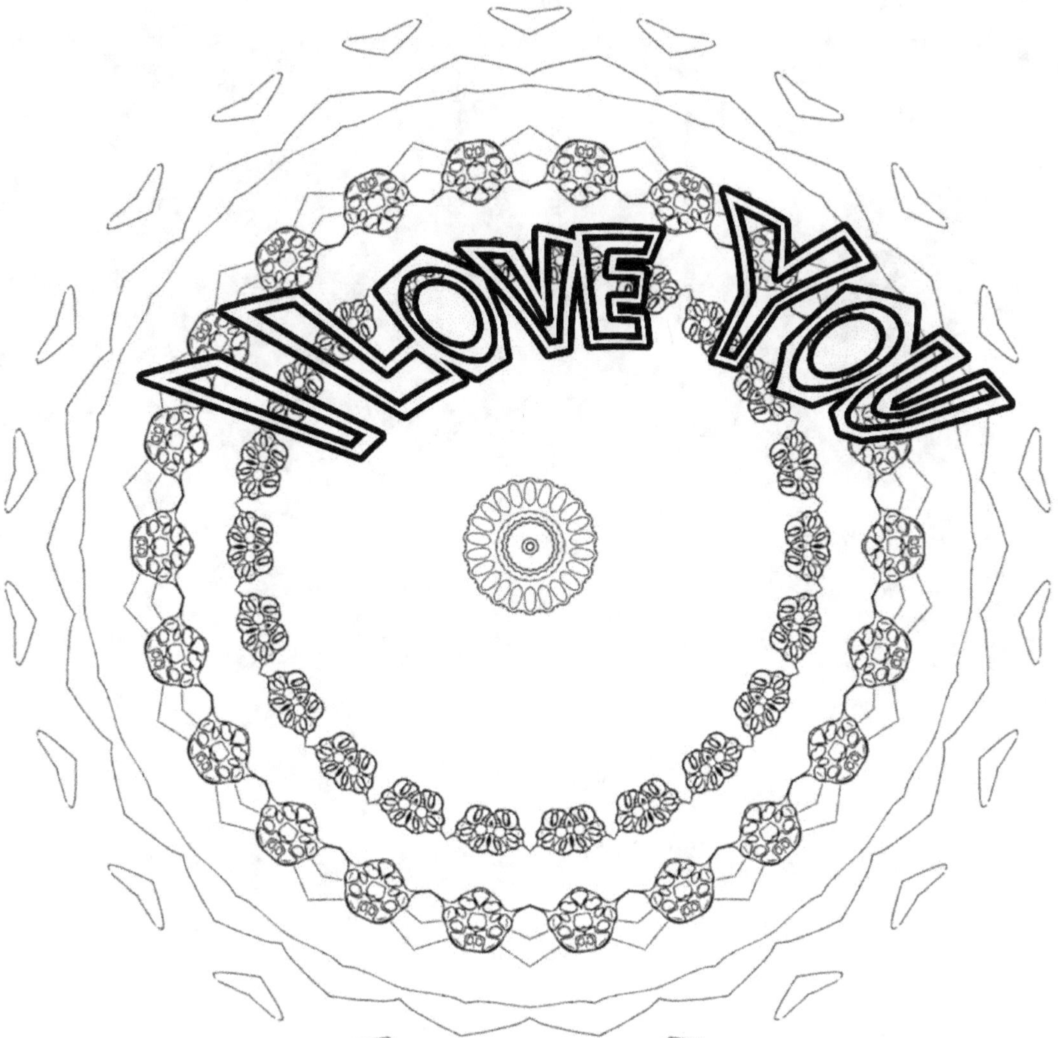
I LOVE YOU

When Love Happen

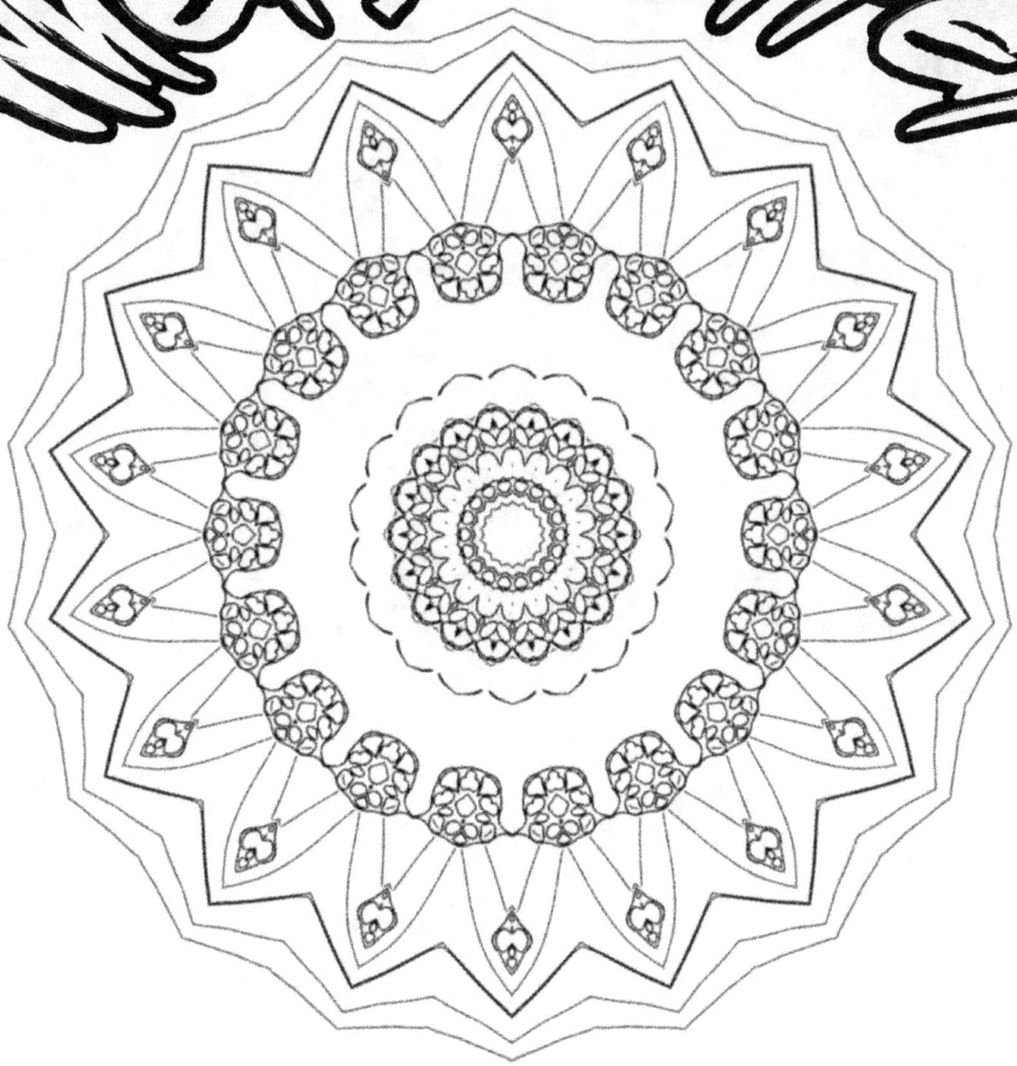

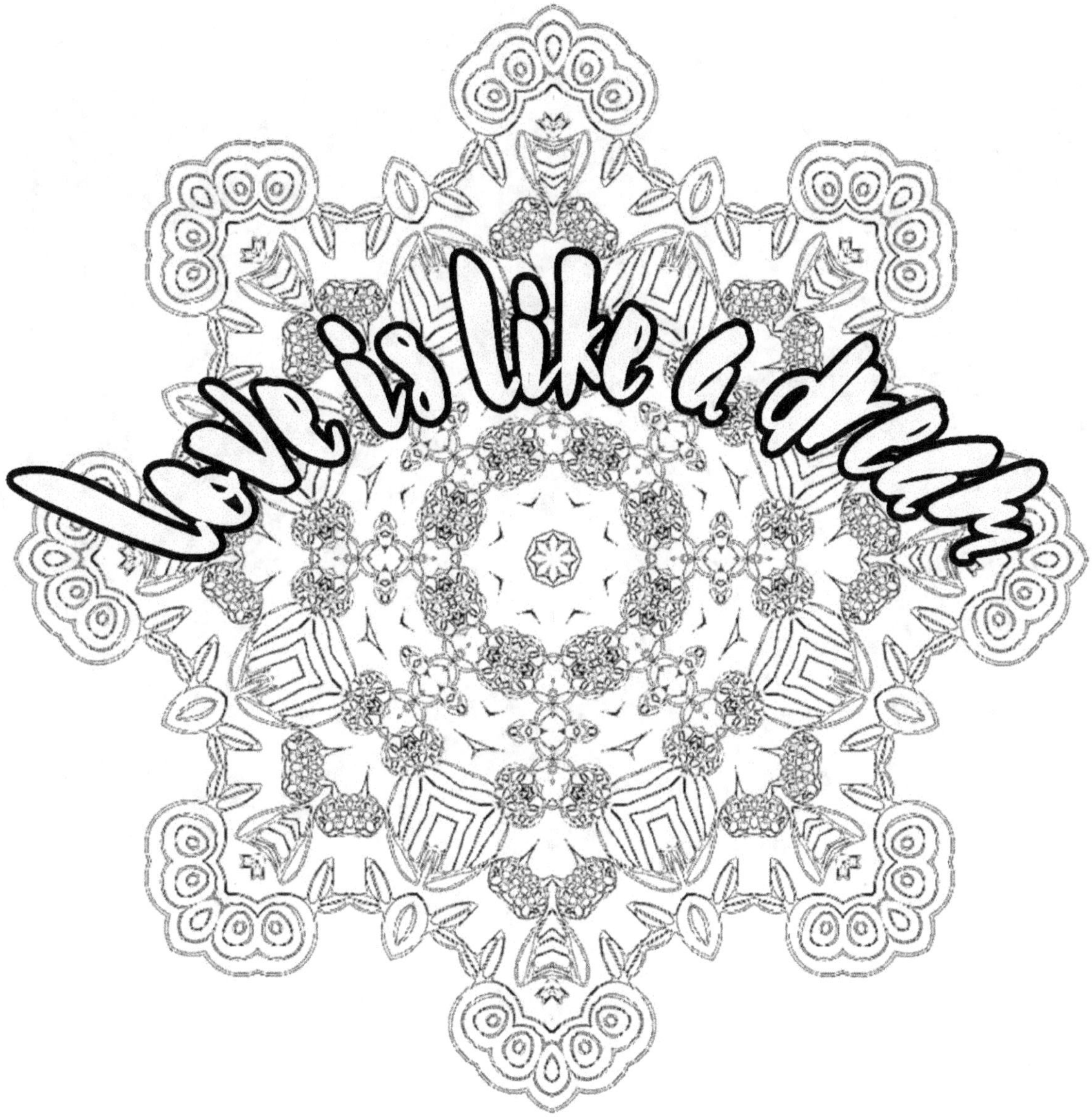
love is like a dream

www.ingramcontent.com/pod-product-compliance
Lightning Source LLC
Chambersburg PA
CBHW081746170526
45167CB00009B/3947